BEAUTY / BEAUTY

Rebecca Perry was born in 1986 in London. She graduated from Manchester's Centre for New Writing in 2008 and lives in London. She has published several pamphlets, including *little armoured* (Seren, 2012), which won the Poetry Wales Purple Moose Prize and was a Poetry Book Society Pamphlet Choice; *cleanliness of rooms and walls* (If a Leaf Falls Press, 2017); *insect & lilac* (2019), co-authored with Amy Key from a joint residency at Halsway Manor (the National Centre for Folk Arts); and *beaches* (Offord Road Press, 2019). Her first book-length collection, *Beauty/Beauty* (Bloodaxe Books, 2015), a Poetry Book Society Recommendation, won the Michael Murphy Memorial Prize 2017, and was also shortlisted for the T.S. Eliot Prize, the Fenton Aldeburgh First Collection Prize and the Seamus Heaney Centre for Poetry Prize for First Full Collection. Her second book-length collection, *Stone Fruit* (Bloodaxe Books, 2021), is a Poetry Book Society Recommendation.

REBECCA PERRY

BEAUTY/BEAUTY

BLOODAXE BOOKS

Copyright © Rebecca Perry 2015

ISBN: 978 1 78037 145 0

First published 2015 by
Bloodaxe Books Ltd,
Eastburn,
South Park,
Hexham,
Northumberland NE46 1BS.

www.bloodaxebooks.com
For further information about Bloodaxe titles
please visit our website and join our mailing list
or write to the above address for a catalogue.

Supported using public funding by
ARTS COUNCIL
ENGLAND

Cover design: Neil Astley & Pamela Robertson-Pearce.

Digital reprint of the 2015 Bloodaxe Books edition.

for
Mum
Dad
&
Mark

ACKNOWLEDGEMENTS

With thanks to the following publications where a number of these poems, or earlier versions of them, have been published: *The Best British Poetry 2013* (Salt Publishing, 2013), *Best Friends Forever* (The Emma Press, 2014), *B O D Y*, *BroadCast*, *CAST: The Poetry Business Book of New Contemporary Poets* (2014), *For Every Year*, *Iota*, *Jarg Magazine*, *The Manchester Review*, *Modern Poets on Viking Poetry: A cultural translation project for Cambridge University*, *Poetry & Audience*, *Poetry London*, *The Poetry Paper* (Aldeburgh Poetry Festival), *Poetry Wales*, *The Quietus*, *The Rialto*, *The Salt Anthology of New Writing* (Salt Publishing, 2013), *Smiths Knoll*, and *What We Heard from the Sea: An Anthology* (Nightbird Press, 2014). Some poems also appeared in a pamphlet, *little armoured*, published by Seren in 2012.

With love and thanks to Mum, Dad, Mark and Ross; to Manchester's Centre for New Writing class of 2007-08, particularly Xiena Saeed, Jason Lee Norman, Matt Munday and Laura Webb (my soup sister); to the Poetry Trust; to John McAuliffe and Roddy Lumsden; to Crispin Best, Amy Key and, most of all, to Alex MacDonald.

CONTENTS

I ▪ THE HUMAN HEART IS CURVED LIKE A ROAD

Pow

Though I think of you   eating three tiny chicken hearts on a skewer
or the skinny girl at school   with shallow breathing and white hands,
chicken-hearted means easily frightened,   and has nothing to do with the heart.

A Crown prince is a male heir to a sovereign throne.   A Crown princess
is the wife of a Crown prince.

Though I think of opening our door to a postman we were told had died
the month before,   postman's knock is a game where imaginary letters
are exchanged for kisses
          and has nothing to do with dead men at the door.

Inner man – the soul or mind, the stomach.   For inner woman see
INNER MAN.   Camelopard is not a hybrid of a camel and a leopard.

Though I think of a line of cow hearts   strung up by the
side of a road in Kochin, blurry with flies, their tubes open to the sky   like bird mouths,
a purple heart is nothing but an amphetamine   or a US military decoration.

Simplicity   is a rainbird.   A rainbird is a bird that can forewarn of rain.

Butter-and-eggs is not butter and eggs,   but a plant with two shades of yellow in
its flower. Daffodil, toadflax, bunny mouths, dead men's bones,   impudent lawyer,
Jacob's ladder, lion's mouth, snapdragon.

Though I am listing flowers   I am not thinking of flowers.

Flowers, Love etc

Many times I've become lost
and snapped out of it next to a rose bush
and bins in someone's front garden
or by a four-way crossing, car horns
and my mouth is full of boring questions.
Many times I've become lost
and found myself helpless as a snow globe
on a mantelpiece in unforgiving sun.

When I kiss someone new my mouth
hosts the ghost mouths of old loves.
A TV static mouth, a cigarette mouth,
a mouth full of piano air and its own ghosts.
And when I touch someone new my hands
are full of grass from all the countries
I've visited alone.

If you look hard enough at any flower
it can resemble some part of the human body.
All living things are busy imitating each other
and while my tongue attempts shadows
of a poppy petal and my navel is a rosebud
I've become lost again on my lookout for a
lost soul who also doesn't believe in souls.

Other Clouds

driving with my father   he said
it is important to see someone die   to help you understand what life is
to help you understand the things   you can do to make it easier
when it has to happen to you   he said
maybe it will rain   it's important to know
the different clouds by sight   it is valuable to predict the weather
he said   remember, if you get married
to pick a ring bigger than your finger   because your fingers,
like your mother's,   swell slightly in the heat
he said   remember we don't
have good knees in this family   you should exercise more
he said   try to settle on a philosophy
it is important to know whether   you want to do life carefully
or thought by thought, as it comes   he said
cut down on the adjectives   people have eyes
he said   remember to pick a hot drink
you can order when pressed for time   don't be the person
holding up the queue   he said
always wear a watch   he said
wind down the window a bit   i want to smell the sea
he said   try to eat more fish
if I got all the bones out   would you eat more
he said   i fancy a pint
i'm glad you can hold your drink   he said
are you in fifth gear yet   does that still make you nervous
he said   it wasn't fair
that men used to have to stay outside   when women gave birth
he said men need   to see life happen
that that's important too   just as much
he said he was glad   I never grew taller than him
he said   that sometimes he still
went to hold my hand   when we crossed the road

Wasp

little lion. little nibbler.
little face dunker. little duck.
little clinging cashew nut.
little sifter, sifting for gold.
little hovercraft. little clamberer.
little engine. little warrior, little armoured.
little yellow-black armadillo.
little snail-slime wings.
little nuzzler, nuzzling a neck.
little alien, little feeler, little zebra.
little dinosaur legs.
little sycophant. little mounter.
little vampire, little pollen sucking bead.
little pocket knife.

Alabaster Baby

Walking from museum to museum
almost crying in each one

in front of an oil painting of a bowl of fruit

in front of a tiny suit of armour

in front of a glass display box of locusts
treading all over each other

in front of a fossilised dinosaur dropping
pink and grey like a pork pie
split in two and varnished

in front of a stuffed pygmy marmoset
hugging the smallest branch

in front of a reconstructed typical Tudor kitchen
with taxidermied chickens and plastic bread

in front of hairpins and pots
a beautifully chiseled miniature family
with a glowing baby you can see light through

in front of the cake selection in the café

in front of a mummy with hair on its feet
a sign that says in 1902 it was publicly
unwrapped and the bandages given
to audience members as souvenirs

in front of various instruments for
torture and castration dented with use
an animatronic man cowering in the corner

in front of a series of mosaics
depicting erotic scenes from ancient Rome

in front of a life-size marble effigy
of a girl about my age
her hands forced into prayer
I want to lean in and kiss her cold lips

A prayer for the wild at heart kept in cages

It's been said that a line can be straight,
or a street, but the human heart
is curved like a road through mountains.
If that's the case I hope a row of goats
are walking over me on my way to you,
otherwise wouldn't that journey be lonely?
And that same person said
when so many are lonely as seem to be lonely,
it would be inexcusably selfish to be lonely alone.

If it's also been said that time
is the longest distance between two places,
does that mean our bodies have been three years apart,
which is greater than the thousands of miles of sea between us,
but you're as real to me as the ground I'm walking on
and the trains I ride to work and back?

And if in memory,
everything happens to music,
what would have been playing as you drank a small beer
with your bare feet on the carpet of a pub floor?
Two new fish in a vast ocean swimming side by side,
sniffing out a new continent. I have no idea.

The violets in the mountains have broken through the rocks.
I don't know how they did it,
but I'm happy for them,
for gentle things to be victorious
even in the name of destruction.
If I got rid of my demons, I'd lose my angels.

Romantic love is beautiful. How easily it is broken.
All cruel people describe themselves
as paragons of frankness. They shout
We don't love you any more! as the rest of us
run into the sea. What else are you supposed to do
on this earth but catch whatever comes to you,
with all your fingers, until your fingers are broken?

I am looking at you through nondescript music again.
Add to that the distortions of my own ego.
How cloudy the glass has become.
I don't tell the truth, I tell what ought to be the truth,
to myself as much as to you.

It has been said that there's a time for departure
even when there's no certain place to go.
We all live in a house on fire
with no fire brigade to call.
I suppose that just leaves the top floor window
and a queen-sized duvet to break the fall.

The paragons of frankness are shouting again.
This time *Life is an unanswered question!*
and now we shout back
But let's still believe in the dignity and importance of the question!

Failing everything else, there's always
the eating of an unwashed grape as a romantic means of dying.
And there's always a handsome man
with a moustache and a large silver watch
if you're prepared to look hard enough.

And since we're all sentenced to solitary confinement
inside our own skins,

and since physical beauty is transitory,
we should all learn to live with it.
Then close the door on it
when the time comes that you look in the mirror
and realise that what you see is all that you will ever be.
And then you accept it.
Or you stop looking in mirrors.

II ■ MY SKIN IS

Sweetheart, come

All the tea and buttered toast in the world is not enough.
All the beaches with their sandy beating hearts and their glittery
shores are not enough. Hold up your boots. Check for mud.
There is no mud. Walk right on through. This is not enough.
Not your adorable dog wanting to be my friend. My god I want that
too. Not a sweater the colour of a Christmassy satsuma, which is
the most particular orange. Not most love which is weak like the
crumbling root of a grey tooth, or the Georgian windows or the plants
that welcome you home like a litter of green tongued puppies. The
couple who can walk and kiss at the same time and not lose
balance, not even. Not even the sad panda at the zoo chewing
into something resembling happiness. Finally! Not guessing first
time round which is the soft eye of the coconut. The friendliest
looking lemon cake in all the world, dedicated to you and you alone,
is not enough. Not your scratchcard or the fruit flies hovering
around a bowl of sweet brown bananas and snow-peaked
oranges. Not that. Just sweetheart come to me in a swarm of insects
pulsing through the sky. Sweetheart come and settle at a place near me.

Windows

(for Alex)

She is opening tab after tab on her laptop screen
so the one with his name in it gets smaller and smaller,
squeezed down by little pieces of the internet
until he is just three letters in the corner,
a peep of light, the last Tetris block before death.

He said that if her arms had grown really long
for whatever reason he'd have carried them down the street
like a train. He said she reminded him
of a statue in Rome that had him in raptures.
He had a photo of it framed.

What's the use of trying to be pretty and dreaming
of ridiculous dresses when love is just an apple
being eaten from the inside?
And now she's tearing up a post-it note and making it rain
bright pink into the bin. Is this what heartbreak feels like –
like rain falling through your head?

All she wants is to see the collection of walking sticks
from Tutankhamun's tomb. To be in Egypt on the deck of a boat
in a cold pool, completely alone, and fine with it.

In the bath, she rolls over and over.
She stands behind the glass balcony door surveying
the windows of the highrise opposite, the lives behind them.
The lights extinguish one by one, to a gallery of frames
with the paintings stolen, and a walled-in quiet.

Over/wintering

the water came from the taps/ yellow
like chicken broth/the wind moved
through the windows as if the glass
wasn't even there/you looked out
of the window, over my shoulder,
at the icy trees/I looked at
your chest & saw your heart
chewing itself/the water wouldn't
run clear/I bathed under a ceiling
of almost dropping brown stars
/it was a dirty-veined house &
poisoned/in the night's blue
silhouettes we remade each
other from the nose
out like a painting

The woman in the sun, a letter

I want my feet to tingle with cold again.
I want you to put your hands between my thighs in bed,
and I would clench them tight for you,
like daisies in a flower press.
I want to press my nipples onto your shoulder blades,
and leave tiny licks of saliva on your back, cold as skis.

I am full of tears.
All day they roll out of my eyes
and fizz to nothing by my feet.
They splash my chest and for a second it is dark there,
then no. I am dry. I am a pillar of salt.

My body is warmed from the inside out.
My stomach is molten inside me,
my lungs bubble from the heat of it.
My heart in your hand would be like
taking a potato straight from the oven,
my bones are the wood of a campfire,
my skin is bed sheets slept in for a day and night.

A Guide to Love in Icelandic

When lemon drops stick together in a paper bag
it's like love.
There are certain risks in cooperative living,
warmth, gravitational laws, the sticky sun.

And when the light bulb pops and explodes
it's like love.
When we are naked and heart pounding in the shower,
in the new dark, afraid of being so close to water.

And it's like love
when the sun disappears for months
and when you stick cloves into an orange.

And when, in the woods, antlers fall from deer onto grass
it's like love.
To persist into spring when you have lost
some part of the whole self.

When you feel a chill and cover your feet
it's like love.
Suddenly you're in a movie, the breeze from an open
window isn't real, the walls are paper, the food is plastic.

And it's like love
when a train stops dead in a tunnel
and when a beloved cat shows its claws.

And when tar is compressed into uniform blocks
it's like love.
The air is all white smoke and impossible to breathe,
the blocks stack to the sky.

When you fall down the stairs
it's like love
and when you are soaked through to the bones,
your clothes are deadweight and the radiators click to life.

Kintsugi 金継ぎ

You said I treated you like a dog,
stroking through your hair
and down over your ears,
and that's what can turn kindness bad.
I would apologise,
but love is the soft parts of us.

*

There is a Japanese word to describe
the sense a person has upon meeting
another person that future love
between them is inevitable.
This is not the same as love at first sight.
For example,
your smell was never unfamiliar.

*

You asked *How can a human being
be so much like a leaf?*
I became infuriated by your questions,
but it's true my veins are alarming
in the shower, blue and desperate
to find each other.
There is a German word
to describe the blue of veins,
which is also grey metal and green
and the colour of haunted houses.

*

There is a Japanese word meaning
to repair broken pottery with gold.

*

Two days alone and I'm talking
to the chilli plant – watching the red
seep through the last green one
like a limb coming to life.
I never noticed how long the light bulbs
take to be bright. I also realise I don't know
the way anywhere. The streets
always just appeared before.

*

The sky is darkening.
How to explain the sadness
I feel in winter, which is a sadness
inextricable from winter.
A sadness specific to the cold,
which sickens my skin.
Winter-sorrow,
when the bed is an iceberg at sea.

*

Of course your preferences present
themselves quietly in the layouts
of rooms. The few things you left
are shadowy objects at the
edges of a Renaissance painting,
waiting to catch the light
when I'm weak.

*

There is a Cheyenne word for the act
of preparing your mouth to speak.
The months spent readying mine
tasted like metal,
food was unpleasant to chew.

*

I look at a bunch of grapes in the bowl
and even their refusal to grow alone
is nature's unnerving bell clanging out
when I'm trying to sleep
in the afternoon.

*

The feeling of remembered love
is so easy to put in the oven and heat up.
It's your ears I long for
when my hands are empty.

III ■ LICKING THE FLAVOUR

The boy

in a verruca sock
made you cry.
You still remember
his goosebumpy arms
against yours in the tight
queue for diving practice
his almost concave torso
and the pink toes
of one foot curved in
the middle like prawns
ready to push away.
The girls were already
starting to feel awkward
in swim suits
hands hovering
like hornets over bodies
not quite landing
on any particular place.

Django Fontina

I saw rain in Galilee.
I saw rain in Lauterbrunnen.
In the Black Forest
apple-sized hailstones
smashed through the windscreens
of abandoned cars.

In Egypt, from a hot air balloon,
I saw a funeral –
a body in a white sheet
lowered into the sand. In Hong Kong,
a man covered in bees.
In Italy, the international space station
flew by three nights in a row,
becoming unremarkable.

Hello, Little Bird

(for Xiena)

You hate that the sun's always out,
even when it rains,
and all you want is to be cold.

It is like a bee behind a curtain
that won't fly out of the window,
can't find its way out of the room.

You say that sometimes
you wish the sun would fuck off and die,
then feel bad for wishing that.

If I tell you it's raining here,
you ask how much rain. You see snow
on the news and it makes you sad.

You have started taking pictures.
The bougainvillea across your sister's face –
two exposures of two lovely things.

You send me a picture of a rubber duck
on a windowsill – one perfect half
of bright orange beak, bright yellow body

and the other half bleached almost grey.
You say the sun is a big tongue;
it is licking the flavour from everything.

You say a boy you went to school with
jumped from a roof, that heroin there
feels like a ghost no one will believe in,

even though it is moving things
in front of your eyes and throwing knives
across the kitchen.

You haven't worn socks
since you left here and you miss the feelings
of wet feet and puddles and rubber soles.

You send me a picture
of the view from your window
and your room, from the doorway.

You send me a picture
of you in a boat, holding a line.
Turns out I'm a terrible fisherman. I don't mind.

I send you a picture of the sign
in Vauxhall you couldn't believe was real.
Tethered balloon ride, 500 metres.

You will come here again in spring.
You ask if you can take photos of me
in the prime of my life.

Ergonomics

I have a soft bread roll on my desk   which two or three times
I've squeezed   very gently   when no one is looking
butter   sprinkle of salt   pea soup   dream
the price of gold is falling   I can't see a window but the reflection
on the floor suggests   intermittent sun   later
I will sit on the church steps   and read   last week
a pigeon actually flew into my chest   an avocado on my desk
is playing dead and prehistoric   another energy giant
has behaved terribly   later   I will take an online IQ test
and do better   turns out the sky is falling down
in fat pieces   later   I will be caught in a vicious cycle
of removing strawberry pips from my teeth   with strawberries
later   moving through the rain texting a person
who is not the person I love   I will be electric in the sweet world

Junk Mail

He bent down to pick a flower but it vanished – at this
       PASSWORD REMINDER. DONATION CONFIRMED. COME TO BED.
she began to cry. He lay down on the bed, heard the click
       WILL YOU HAVE A BABY? FREE PSYCHIC READING SENT TO YOU!
of the door. Saw a red carpet. Then the sun itself plucked
       GO THE EXTRA MILE: TAKE A POSTGRADUATE COURSE OVERSEAS.
up courage. Friend, be very sure of this. Bees were coaxed
       STEAK OR LOBSTER DINNER FOR TWO WITH LIVE JAZZ/
out of hives like blood drops. At this she began to cry.
       LASER TEETH WHITENING. WEEKEND LINE AND STATION CLOSURES.
She said, My Heart's A Balloon. It is going to burst.
       IF YOU HAVE SUFFERED A BEREAVEMENT. BE A BETTER LOVER.
I am sure of this much – it is going to get caught in a tree.
       THE QUANTITY THEORY OF INSANITY. GREY AREA. VITAL BEAUTY.

immortelle

at the time of writing a single apple costs 45p
the writer is sleeping well

at the time of writing
the glasses in the cabinet have never been quieter

the writer is thinking of eating her own hands
at the time of writing all

blueberries appear to be shipped in from Spain
the writer dreams of millionaires with blue teeth

her childhood friends in white theatre masks
the bones of their feet

the valley of cherries in Ljubljana
that keeps the whole country well-stocked in cherries

but the writer dreams them as tiny blood buds
which is to destroy the image

at the time of writing the boundless joy
of a pre-walk dog is suggesting itself in the writer's chest

a bruise the size and colour of a grape
intensifies on her thigh

at the time of writing the writer is thinking
of composing a painting and a subject is needed

a reclining night sky? canyons of fruit trees?
an abandoned baby bear?

* * *

the writer is running her fingers
over the carvings of an Egyptian temple

so much past seems absolutely impossible
it later deflates her to learn

that the temple has been moved from the original site
the experience now seems less valid

* * *

at the time of writing the writer refuses to believe
she will ever die, as the flowers in the streets

refuse the same, as too do those in homes,
parks, cemeteries, places we cannot see

* * *

at the time of writing the days are wide as lakes
and often deeper

the writer feels verbose and embarrassed
by her overwhelmingly positive experience of life

while travelling for a writing project
the writer meets another writer

seeking refuge from his home country
which was no longer a safe place for him to write

the writer drinks beer with the writer
she searches his eyes for something

when she asks if he misses his home
searching for herself in him atrociously

and he says not home, his family
the writer asks when will he see them again

and the writer answers he cannot imagine when
he talks about home still as my country

the writer cannot imagine ever using these words
in her hostel room the writer cries

loudly over the bathroom sink
which is full of cherries soaking in water.

IV ■ WHEN A DOG GOES TO HEAVEN
THE STARS ARE GREEN

All the Sad Movies

In the forest, in spring, the graves are green
and broken – graves for dogs, warrior's graves,
graves of men and women, a trilogy of children.

Flowers, a single flower, nests, a broken doll,
pyjamas, a spring of reds, a winter of dark.
Sarah and Lilya 4eva.

In winter, the snow in the forest is a peppermint
beach. In winter, colour is broken.
The striped deer are gone, the magnolias
are gone. The cuckoo is finding heaven.

In autumn, the trees are scissor hands.
On the trees, in red, *Leon et Maude.*

In a perfect world, in summer, the hunter
and the deer are 50/50.
In a perfect world Sarah and Lilya are 4eva.

In a perfect world, all dogs go to heaven.
When a dog goes to heaven the stars are green.

Baba Ghanoush

Just here, you said, pointing
to the patch of grass beside your boots.
A frost had crawled over the ground
and night was tilting in.

The names I gave my pets
when I was small are a constant
reminder of my innate ordinariness.
I wondered what kind of child you'd been
to name yours so spectacularly.
You placed a sparkler in the earth
and we watched its orange pip slip down
to its fretful end, then quietly
crunched back to the house, sharing a
pocket, the cold in our throats,
the sky handsome as an aubergine.

Inside, you dedicated yourself
to the reconstruction of a miniature
Battersea Power Station in stainless steel.
Night crouched down over the house,
put its rigid arms around us. They
were cold, hard-edged like cutlery.
Between two curtains the ground outside
was a million silver spiders playing dead
and I couldn't look at them. What
were we but stupid animals, frightened
of our own stretching shadows.

The Pet Cemetery

Our darling Wolf,
you passed so peacefully.
Crow, my sunbeam.
Bobbit, my consolation.
Pomme de Terre, we were such friends.
Life is very lonely without you.

Fattie, my joy.
Ponto. See you on the other side.
We had twelve years together, Chips,
I will never forget.
My adorable Scum.
I.M.U., my relentless Casper.
My most magnificent Baron,
where have you gone?

In loving memory of Ruby Heart.
I.L.M. Jim.
Mousse, keep chasing cats.
Cutie, keep catching birds.
Mr Beak, now you're free to fly.

Orphie, at the end of this lonely life
I'll see you at the Golden Gate.
Darling Pippin.
Gentle Drag.
Tender Scamp, you will never be replaced.
Warmhearted Trix,
you were the salt of the earth.
Teddy, you aristocrat.
Keep living the high life.

Dear Stegosaurus

Bus-sized and gentle, you are master of peace,
diplomacy, berries, grass, perseverance, pace.

Your warm, rough belly sags with majesty over ferns,
cycads and dust. Your spikes are dull and magnificent,

a row of abandoned kites, rusted by a tough winter,
in a tree stripped of guts. You're not a fighter, though

you will fight. It's hard to just stay out of trouble
when everyone else is looking for it, I know. Tinted red

and armoured, I think I couldn't know more beauty
if I travelled the earth ten thousand times.

The perfections of your tiny head trounce a sunset,
your mouth holds more wonder than a sky full of stars.

Pepo

Her imaginary friend died on the morning
of her eighth birthday and what a lesson to learn
as her living friends screeched in the garden
like mosquitoes, wearing down the grass
with their flashing shoes and the balloons
stared back at her with furious shining eyes.
Her cake was a castle she cut into pieces
with a butter knife. She ate the tower her
imaginary friend would have lived in, and left
her tower where it was, a symbol of her solitude.

To mark a week since that day,
she takes a watermelon to their favourite spot
by the pond, where they first met, under a roof
of trees. She sits on the froggy leaves, carves
the watermelon into pieces, feels the ache
of something irreversible happening with each
crack of its skin, senses her heart becoming baggy.
She imagines she is cutting up the world, blasting
an atlas to its edges. She places the continents
in separate spots around the pond's edge,
then leaves them to contemplate this
new state of being, the insurmountable water.

The Year I Was Born:
the day by day chronicle of events in the year of your birth

January, frosty month,
the Challenger explodes 74 seconds after lift-off.
A motorway in Bavaria closes for 7 hours
after a lorry turns over
and spills 24 tonnes of noodles.

February, the month of cakes,
a perfect black tulip is grown in Holland
after 25 years of failed attempts.
February 9th, new moon.

March, boisterous month,
the American wonder lemon is harvested,
producing an eggcupfull of juice when squeezed.
Halley's Comet travels in a huge orbit
around the sun
and won't return again until I am 76.

April, the opening month, fool's May –
the Royal Mint is 1100 years old,
Texas is 150 years old,
the Biro is 40 years old,
the Berlin wall is 25 years old.
April 24th, total eclipse of the moon.

May, blossoming month,
poor weather wipes out over half of Britain's beehives.
From this month onwards all new phones
will have push buttons rather than dials.
A radiaoactive cloud
from Chernobyl reaches England.

June, dry month,
the rarest buttercup in Britain goes on show.
Admiral Horatio Nelson gets ready
to have his face washed.
The pier at Southend is sliced in two by a sludge ship.

July, the yellow month.
July 6th, new moon.
For her 100th birthday,
the Statue of Liberty has her nose rebuilt
and her insides cleaned with sodium bicarbonate.
2,000 lobsters escape
when a lorry turns over at Bere Regis, Dorset.

August, month of harvest,
5 large teddy bears fall off a lorry on the M3
and are taken into custody at Basingstoke police station.
Southend Pier is mended.

September, barley month, holy month,
new moon September 4th.
Hundreds of people in Paris
demonstrate outside the pets' cemetery
which is threatened with closure.

October, month of the winter moon,
over 3 tonnes of mixed biscuits block the road
for 7 hours in Markeaton, Derbyshire,
after a lorry turns over.
The Jonagold apple, a cross between a Jonathan
and a Golden Delicious,
is voted most eatable apple of the year.

November, slaughter month, the month of blood.
A raindrop 8 millimetres in diameter
is found in a cloud just east of Hawaii.
A 124,000,000-year-old dinosaur,
found in a Surrey claypit,
is officially named *Baryonyx Walkeri*,
meaning 'a heavy clawed creature found by Mr Walker'.

December, dead month, month of yule.
December 1st, new moon.
December 16th marks the beginning of mince pie season.
December 31st, second new moon.

V ■ SOME PEOPLE ARE SAID TO BE SLEEPLESS

My grandfather considers his life in three stages

Matrimony, two children, some bad things.
He has stood tall and unshaking like the dead apple tree
at the end of his garden. He has forged himself deep –
never moving far; making occasional trips
to local places, the garden, to see family if he has to.
He looks out at the sky from his front room window,
through the net curtains. His eyes say he is waiting
for the mob to come and unceremoniously dismantle him,
pillar by pillar, plucking out the sacred stone
at the centre of his body and smashing it to pieces
against the wall. They will leave one stone to mark the spot.
One stone to stand as the promise of a man that was,
which is better than the reality, he says,
which after all, wasn't so great.

Posted to Italy, Africa, another place
whose name has now changed. He remembers fires,
and heat even in the dead of night. Everything simmered,
small fires hopped from place to place
like rabbits from hutch to hutch. He never fired a gun.
At night, counted flaming sheep, thought of his wife,
at home, heating the house with coals. He never fired a gun
but people were still dead, scattered around.
He felt not so much that he was melting but that
perhaps his bones were thinning from the inside out.
He vowed never to leave England again
and never did. This stage ended not with a great fire
or explosion but with a gentle collapse
of buckling ash and a distinct sense of conceding.

The assembling of himself, piece by piece,
a tiny construction. He has a short film in his mind
of his own creation. He plays it over and over. It is not
a slow process of growth, but his bones coming together
like synchronised swimmers, slotting into place perfectly.
Then, a feeling of strength, being freshly born each day.
Of a good and solid structure – a constant energy,
tiny bees under his skin. His arms and legs were small,
mighty columns – capable of stopping the sky from falling.
His eyes, an excellent brown like freshly dug earth after rain,
would look directly at the sun, taking everything in.
This stage was short and ended all too suddenly –
washed away like twigs in strong water
one night when he was sleeping, and he woke.

Shifting

All of us crammed in there
like buffalo standing before water at nightfall, looking ahead.
All of us shadows and shapes, quietly shifting.
      That day being your face, and the constant threat of rain,
the air seeming thick as the ground.   Your face
         being the saddest thing I have ever seen.
Then the weight of our footsteps
           outside the church.
The soft tread of us, our press into the grass;
      temporary craters on soft earth and proof of us being alive,
a dissatisfied herd breathing quietly, waiting to act as one.

Phonograph

She was held by a rope
to a tall pole on the beach
and what a nightmarish thought
with the strong wind and the
smoky clouds. Some people,
like some animals,
are said to be sleepless,
which the sea never is
and not the mind, either.

Her knees bend and her
eyes close in forgetting –
there's always something.
She remembers that some of
the beasts at the sale
were tied by the nose to posts
and now it's too late to help.
She would wish to make
the storm a calm if she had
the power to wish anything.

Last Sunday he said:
to be of use ought to be
the aim of our lives.
To look at the stars on a clear
evening is to be impressed
by their number and the
immensity of space. Lastly,

the masters of all, whoever
they are, are blessed to
possess wisdom many
ages older than ours.
They long, like ourselves,
to flash across space a signal
of life and fellowship.

Casida of the Dead Sun

the earth reedless, a pure form,
closed to the future

FEDERICO GARCÍA LORCA:
'Casida of the Recumbent Woman'

The world is in the process of ending.
The insects have dropped from the air.

The last wasp is sinking through
the gloopy green water of a garden pond,
the most melancholy diver.

The sun is on its back at the very top
of the sky, floating bleakly, jelly-eyed.

A toad's heart is blinking inside
its nobbly body as it contemplates
the infinite civilisations of the world,

the disappointment of having
only ever truly known this one.

The Glass Boat

We ate peaches on a balcony
above the dirtiest
car park you can imagine.

The sea was a slice
at the bottom of the sky.
The undersides of our feet

were powdery grey and we
idled, making a treasure map
of our bedroom floor.

When we took a slow walk
through the village with its
warm fish blood smell and

houses bearded with purple
flowers, the small dogs
without homes made me sad,

which isn't to mention
the small cats without homes
that did the same to you

(my companion).
Later we watched the tide
lick away a declaration

of love in the sand.
And then, the next bright
morning, our tiny guide

led us through the hidden
currents of a gorge, then into
a chest-deep stretch,

the water rushing, holding
our bags up above his head.
We had never known

water so greedy,
or our bodies so pathetic
and betrayed. The little

black stones cut into
our shins and the tops
of our feet. Blood puffed

out into the white water,
trailing behind us, then onto
tissue, like roses. I wore

nothing under my sundress
on the drive back and the air
flowed around underneath it

(my mischievous friend).
That early evening,
we looked down through

the glass bottom
of a small boat, drinking
cold bottled beer.

The shock of the morning
was a goosebumpy
memory, the sleepy water

below us was a lie and the
unbelievable silver of the fish
didn't belong to our world,

as they streamed
and streamed past,
a sudden influx of robots.

Hungry

I have so often felt bad for the sea.
The so relentlessly destined sea,
the inexorable sea,
the unable to say *Kiss me here and here*
or *Please, I just want to sleep* sea.

I misread Akheilos,
the shark-shaped sea spirit
as Akheilos, the heart-shaped sea spirit,
such was/is my habit
of seeking love where there is none.

Here is what little girls should
dream of: hair like a mermaid's,
the grace of a dolphin,
jewels, breath that smells of apples.
And haven't I since forever wanted to live
in a cave at the bottom of the ocean?

I am always underwater –
in a swimming pool, running my hand
along its white tiled floor/in a cool,
dark lake rising to the surface/
perhaps I'm pressing the bottoms of my feet
to the surface of a slimy grey dam/
cutting through a calm sea,
parting a shoal of bright red fish.

Underwater, you are in either
the prison or castle
of your own heartbeat,

depending how you feel about
inner workings.

The poor, over-romanticised sea.
The lonely sea calling out for a friend
to go drinking with on a cold,
winter evening. And the sea is hungry,
of course.

It's hard to imagine
the speed of a tortoise's heartbeat
as it hovers in dark water.
And when its heart stops beating,
long after it's dead,
it's hard to imagine its imprint
in a night sky – a constellation
appearing slowly, like a million
brilliant ideas pressing into the mind.

I find it very hard
to believe that drowning
can be a peaceful way to die.

The sea is lonely at Christmas.
And when you watch the rain
hitting the sea it seems
like a great absence returning home,
but who can be sure of any of it –
the inscrutable sea, the sea
like a rusted mirror,
the sea turning its back on you
with a long, disappointed look.

VI ▪ WITH PERFECTLY SYMMETRICAL FACE

The Execution of Lady Jane Grey

Executioner: X
Lady Jane Grey: J

X: In your own time.

J: Yes.

X: You come here to die.

J: This morning was my last morning.

X: I trust you thanked God for it.

J: I am always grateful for waking.

X: What do you have to say?

J: Very little. I am humbled by the way the light is falling on the grass.

X: And in front of these people do you acknowledge the multitude of your sins?

J: I am bound to.

X: We who are left behind will pray for you.

J: I had hoped to see one final bird before the end.

X: There's an edge to the air.

J: Despatch me quickly.

X: This is your life's final transaction.

J: I have never taken pleasure in money.

X: This is a necessity. God will reward you for it.

J: Within reason, a wilting flower is revived with water.

X: The possibilities of the Lord are not bound by reason – you know this.

J: *(pause)* My clothes?

X: Your gown first.

J: Here.

X: Your headdress.

J: Here.

X: You've been told many times, I'm sure, how your hair resembles fire.

J: People have said, the fires of Hell.

X: Your collar.

J: Here.

X: And so…

J: Despatch me quickly.

X: May the Lord flow through the blood and muscle in my arms.

J: And the blade of your axe.

X: And the blade of my axe.

J: I think I am ready.

X: I'm sorry about the birds.

J: Such is the nature of creatures with wings.

X: I ask your forgiveness for this act.

J: You have it.

X: Then place your knees here.

J: We are cursed, we who die on our knees, and few.

X: Should I tie the blindfold?

J: Please don't.

X: For your peace, I recommend it. Move your hair from your neck.

J: I think someone is calling me?

X: The block…

J: What shall I do? Where is it?

On serendipity

Fortuitous happenstance indeed   the way the fresh water stream
bent in the ground at each perfect angle not necessarily required of it
to greet your toes   when the sun was stripped back and hot hot enemy
yes burning   and you felt so desperate and lost   your brain
without instruction began recalling the body and face of the first person
you thought you loved   smell   hair   teeth
hip bone   meeting stomach   sweet spit
at the same time as hard crying   and preparing to die

Then serendipitous too   the way the apples pushed out their shoulders
to fill one hundred shining green coats   hanging from branches
waiting for your aching teeth   your sandy tongue
honey too   there was honey in the trunk
     shade   were you ever more thankful?

And look also   the way the blue of the sky mixes with the yellow
of its sun   now also your sun once again to make
a green   so truly transfixing   as this

Poor Sasquatch

When Sasquatch was found face down on a dual carriageway
the world united in a quiet and shameful silence.

He was moved to a secure location and subjected
to a live autopsy on the Discovery Channel revealing,
like a huge rose, circulatory, muscular and skeletal systems
much like our own but with all the predictable differences.

His stomach contents proved him to be a gentle vegetarian,
foraging on low ground, particularly enjoying
varieties of berries usually poisonous to humans.
A reconstructive video demonstrated how he would have
walked, run and rested.

They put photos of his hands, feet and closed eyes
on the news and as part of an extensive ten-page spread
in a memorial edition of *The Times*.
He was auctioned off to an anonymous bidder.

After public outcry, the anonymous bidder
entered into negotiations with the British Museum.
Plans were put in place to ensure that he would be interred
in such a place to be viewed by the public,
who came in droves to see this thing so long denied to them.
Breathing on the glass and touching
the animatronic model beside the glass case
despite the signs thanking them for not doing so.

In my dreams he followed me around all my life.
When I walked through a shopping centre, he was behind me,
peering in through the shop windows at the colourful cakes,
which he longed for.
And when I walked along a pavement
he was on the traffic side, taking the hits,
the headlights of a million cars setting him on fire.

Exemplifying Grace

Botticelli keeps secrets
Botticelli cries every day
Botticelli sleeps
with the curtains open
for the sky

Botticelli is never certain if the sun
rises or sets in the west
Botticelli exemplifies grace

Botticelli paints breasts very slowly
Venus leaning to the left
Venus with hands on chest
Venus with perfectly symmetrical face

Botticelli hides a boy
they say
he draws him every night
and burns it every morning

Botticelli has specified his burial place
Botticelli dislikes shadows
Botticelli paints
Botticelli possesses linear rhythm

He paints on great church walls
Botticelli gets skinnier

Botticelli paints lamentations
Botticelli paints very quickly
Botticelli paints statues and trees
and annunciations

Character Development of the Lovers

Which part of his body does He lead with and what does this tell us about him?
Leads 8/10 with the groin suggesting sexual aggression/prowess/masculinity.

Which part of her body does She lead with and what does this tell us about her?
Leads 9/10 with chest – indicates promiscuity.

What key facts should we know about The Lovers after their first scene?
He loves her. She doesn't appear to love him.

What do we know about The Wife?
Very little. She is mentioned twice – first when He says she has a strong sense of smell, and finally when She sees a photograph of her, laughs.

What prop is She holding when she first enters and what is its significance?
Enters holding umbrella (it is summer) – suggests irrationality, pessimistic tendencies. Umbrella as an object also practical, phallic.

What colour are the curtains in The Couples' room and what does this tell us about their relationship?
Blue, suggesting a coldness. Could also hint at drowning (son's death is never explained fully, though water is involved).

What colour are the curtains in The Lovers' room and what does this tell us about them?
A neutral, non-suggestive colour such as beige. Also reminiscent of flesh.

If your characters eat, what do they eat?
He eats frequently – mostly cold meat on the bone. She does not eat, but drinks often.

What sound effects will be required, when (and why, if appropriate)?
None, besides the sound of glass smashing during the blackout.

What costume will She/ He be wearing in the final scene and why?
She: Black dress with embellishment around the neckline. He: Black trousers, smart though stained, and shirt with loose tie (to foreshadow hanging).

How should the audience feel upon leaving the theatre?
The audience should feel both hopeful and hopeless, leaving with either a desire to convey to the person they love how much they love them, or to sleep with someone new.

A Most Satisfactory Dreamlife

But what love could be prior to it?
What is prior?
What is love?
My questions were not original.
Nor did I answer them.

ANNE CARSON: 'The Glass Essay'

Night drips its silver tap.
At 4am I wake, silent and brilliantly lit.
The bare blue trees.

My face in the bathroom mirror
is all the ways I hope I am not myself
and discover I am, over and over again.

World as a kind of half-finished sentence.
World as a black night in January.

A thousand questions hit my eyes from the inside.

The man who left first,
his name was Adam.
I hardly remember myself then, or my body.
Our mortal boundaries
grew visible around us like lines on a map.
Such necessity grinds itself out.

Love as eyes, stars, inside, outside, actual weather.
Love as the bars of time, which broke.

I stood on the edge of the conversation,
snow covered us both.
I felt as if the sky was torn off my life.
It made me merciless.

World as I am surrounded by the idiocy of men.
World as *Why all this beating of wings?*
World as *This melon is grainy. Not a good melon.*

In the silent kitchen
I tap a pomegranate free from its skin
with a spoon.
Jewel, spaceship, abundance.

Desolation as watching the year repeat its days.
Desolation as scooping up blue and green lozenges
of April heat a year ago in another country.

A great icicle has formed on the railing of my balcony.
It seems to me like a perfect metaphor for heartbreak,
how it grows.
I am cold and without clothes in the orange light
of the railway line creeping behind my house.
I am not a melodramatic person.

It would be sweet
to have a friend to tell things to at night.
Stored up secrets have etched themselves
inside the ice.

Last week a woman was crying beside me on the bus;
I willed my body to generate heat for her.
This felt like a common reaction.
I tried to wear my own absence of heartbreak lightly.

World as girls are cruellest to themselves.
World as my knees are cold inside my clothes.
World as a blue hole at the top of the sky.

I have a photograph taped to my fridge
of my grandmother.
In the hospital, distinctions tended
to flatten and coalesce.
Biscuits, curtains, closed windows, buzzing light.

Sickness as dreamtails and angry liquids.
Sickness as *I am interested in anger.*

I boil a kettle and carry it to the bath.
The tap gushes out.
I am avoiding my own eyes in the mirror.
It has always seemed unwise to contemplate your face
in the short time following waking.

Promise as the stunning moment one's lover comes in
and says *I do not love you anymore.*
Promise as my heartbeat traveling through the bathwater.

I like to believe that something of the heart of a woman
who lies on her back in the ground
is trembling through the water.

Love as the smell of limes and roses blowing in the window.
The water escapes into the air –
this low, slow collusion.

VII ■ I AM CARGO

Soup Sister

And, of course,
it bothers me greatly that I can't know
the quality of the light where you are.
How your each day pans out,
how the breeze lifts the dry leaves from the street
or how the street pulls away from the rain.

Last week I passed a tree
that was exactly you in tree form,
with a kind look and tiny sub-branches
like your delicate wrists.

Six years ago we were lying
in a dark front room on perpendicular sofas,
so hungover that our skin hurt to touch.
How did we always manage
to be heartbroken at the same time?

I could chop, de-seed and roast
a butternut squash for dinner
in the time it took you to shower.

Steam curtained the windows, whiting out
the rain, which hit the house sideways.
One of us, though I forget who, said
do you think women are treated like bowls
waiting to be filled with soup?
And the other one said, of course.

Now the world is too big,
and it's sinking and rising
and stretching out its back bones.

The rivers are too wild,
the mountains are so so old
and it's all laid out arrogantly between us.

My friend, how long do you stand
staring at the socks in your drawer
lined up neat as buns in a bakery,
losing track of time and your place in the world,
in the (custardy light of a) morning?

____ is transported on a ship from Y to Z

I sleep
with one foot on the floor

I think I will never
shake this rocking out of me

I am cargo
and I am seasick
and at night I see an eye
at the hole in the wall

and it is the eye of the man
the man who is my handler

I am learning
to navigate by a strip of light on the deck
and things aren't
happening fast enough

and my chest heaves
and my sweat is yellow

and there is no way
to make the toothpain go away
besides

oh how many times
must I plait my hair

and I suffer night terrors
and I lack the privacy to be disgusting
and my stomach is angry

and my sweat is brown
and I am promised

I find comfort
in thinking how old is this boat
how old the chirring wood

how old the trees it came from
when planted, when cut

and to piece the trees back together
and name them

how the earth increases

(after the Waking of Angantýr)

She is awake and
how the whole
awake at the same
that case a moment

thinking about
world is never all
time and how in
can never truly be

global and how
interesting for more
people at a time.
to be an assemblage.

things are rarely
than two or three
Simply, our inability
She imagines a gong

with the power
everybody, a gong
everything. She hates
the sleeping fall open

to wake the world,
of unimaginable
how the mouths of
like the mouths

of the dead. She
with keys to the
next to her on the
from the streetlight

thinks of her friend
garden in Soho
grass, the bright orange
across his face. She

thinks of the heart
visualises a silver cage
anger that the signs of
always Someone &

as a mind enclosure,
around it. She feels
small businesses are
Son. She thinks of

aubergines as the
vegetable kingdom.
as horses of the sea.
video in biology of

horses of the
She thinks of ships
Seahorses. That
the male giving birth.

The word spasm.   Tomorrow, the tent
of the sun will be   pitched somewhere
in the sky, as always   ready to be rained on.
Her teacher once   suggested that the

girls should pay   attention to how
the boys conduct   themselves. How they
don't fuss. You think   of yourself as just a
human being until   something happens.

Estrapade

When you turned away   from me in bed that final time,
your back was a cold, white plate   with no food on it. I remembered
the video on the news of the horse   that threw off its rider, then fell down,
but I didn't know if I was the horse   or the rider in this scenario
so my body became a shipwreck instead. When I was small the little mermaid
disappeared into foam on the surface   of the sea and I turned the page
for the bit where she came back   and she never came back.

Poem in which the girl has no door on her mouth

the girl in the bathroom

the way pips are suspended

she spits into the sink

where is this bathroom

from a distance

her heartbeat vibrates little waves

she is an island

in her ears is a fuzzy

a voice from the next room calls out

whose voice is this

there is a pain

it is a central pain

when she closes her eyes

in identical clothes

their purpleness

it is a hot bright day

fills the air or seems to

once again the moment

which will be arrows

who looks at them

the brain tells the body a lie

the heart continues to beat

like a mouth failing

her words are waiting

in the throat of an apple

who is this girl

she throws something into the bin

she very rarely misses

through the bathwater

the sound of her blood

high-pitched sound

come here

what do they want from her

between her shoulder blades

where wings would sprout from

she is in a room of girls

refusing to dissect cow hearts

their unromantic shapes

and the smell of blood

under water she is rehearsing

she will pour forth words

which lodge in the thigh of a warrior

but doesn't feel pain

the brain tells the eyes a lie

after it is removed from the body

over and over again to find words

A Woman's Bones Are Purely Ornamental

We have each been our worst ever kiss
to someone else
on a warm evening,
leaning on the boot of a car,
filling the silence with reams of words,
them asking if you're trying to be strange.

Mine was a hard tongued boy
who I passed into the mouth of a laughing friend
during a demonstration one night of our worst ever kisses.
We slept in front rooms like baby rats
on the floor, covering the carpet.

We learnt tricks
like how to make our collarbones
as prominent as possible
and how to be interested
without being too interesting.

My friend's hands were beautiful,
as were everyone else's.
I looked at them when they tapped pens in maths
or painted PVA glue on their fingers.
The worst parts of ourselves
were the best parts of others, it became increasingly clear.

Our English teacher
had a keen interest in serial killers
and their motives.
He mentioned this twice.

Who can say where one house ends and another begins.
I envied girls with space between their thighs,
with more than three bedrooms in their house.
At night I could hear my neighbour plug
her phone charger into the wall
which was her wall and my wall, both.

To teach myself about nudity
I sculpted a semi-3D likeness of a woman's naked back
using rolled up pieces of newspaper
to make her spine and shoulder blades
rise up from the page.
I ran my fingers over her.

Everyone must feel they're being
outstripped somehow
we were advised often.

In gymnastics we did back flips
repeatedly, in a line, until we were told to stop.
On the first day of a spring term
we found a fox floating in the swimming pool.

We lay down in the snow on the school field
in a star shape, letting ourselves go cold.
We couldn't believe it when teachers returned
from a summer holiday married.

Details of our predecessors were well documented;
the girl who blinded herself with a fretsaw,
the girl who sewed through her own hand,
the girl who set her hair on fire with a Bunsen burner,
the girl who hung herself in the bell tower.

In our final assembly we performed
a musical with lyrics inserted
for the sole purpose of mocking our teachers.
One girl had cuts on her thighs,
one girl was pregnant.
People lost their virginity mostly on sofas
or in the backs of cars.
We were told to make the most of our bodies.

On the school sign we changed
'Independent Day School for Girls aged 3-18'
to 'Independent Day School for Girls Certified Criminally Insane'.
In our final Latin class, our teacher wrote
Crede quod habes, et habes, ladies!
on the chalkboard. He urged us to remember this
as we embarked on our lives as young women.

My friends were all around me, like birds.
Sometimes, in the sun, I remember
how we ungratefully acted out plays on the grass,
our belongings thrown over the backs of chairs
in a hot, shadowy room nearby.

Like this, in the snow
I remember the warmth of touching tongues,
walking towards my friend's car –
a little alien thing, a polar bear's solitude
stamped in four black paws on tarmac –
her hands on the wheel,
our words in white puffs,
what we spoke of.

NOTES

A prayer for the wild at heart kept in cages (16) is inspired by, and quotes from, the various plays, memoirs and interviews of Tennessee Williams.

Phonograph (53) is comprised of phrases taken from Pitman's *Short-hand Instructor.*

Casida of the Dead Sun (55): The epigraph from Federico García Lorca's 'Casida of the Recumbent Woman' is translated by Michael Smith.

A Most Satisfactory Dreamlife (70) is indebted to Anne Carson's *The Glass Essay* from which many of its lines, words and phrases have been taken.